Keto Diet for Beginners 2018

Low Carb, High-Fat Recipes for Losing Weight, Heal Your Body and Regain Confidence (Lose up to 20 Pounds in 3 Weeks)

Dr. Suzanne Wells

Disclaimer Notice:

Please note the information contained within this document is for educational and entertainment purposes only. Every attempt has been made to provide accurate, up-to-date and reliable, complete information. No warranties of any kind are expressed or implied. Readers acknowledge that the author is not engaging in the rendering of legal, financial, medical or professional advice.

By reading this document, the reader agrees that under no circumstances are we responsible for any losses, direct or indirect, which are incurred as a result of the use of information contained within this document, including, but not limited to, errors, omissions, or inaccuracies.

Table of contents

CHAPTER 1: UNDERSTANDING THE KETO DIET

To easily understand the ketogenic diet, it is a diet plan comprising 9ngridients which stimulates the process of ketosis and lets the body use fats as an energy source instead of sugar (glucose). It has numerous health benefits which include increase in mental and physical performance of the body alongside a concrete weight loss. This brief introduction will explain why there are millions of followers of the keto diet and why it is so beneficial.

What happens in your body when you eat keto?

The ketogenic diet stimulates the propagation of ketones in the body. These ketones bodies are further used as a fuel for the human body instead of sugar. The 'keto' portion of the word 'ketogenic' is explained by this. These ketones are used as a fueling source while there is a lower presence of sugar in the body.

Ketone production is inversely proportional to carbs intake, the lower the carb consumption; the higher will be the production of ketones. They can be conveniently divided into blood sugar (glucose) and a moderate amount of proteins. It is important to understand that high protein intake can also result into production of glucose.

Ketones are mainly produced by fats and are present inside the liver. The energy produced by ketones is used for the entire functioning of the body including the brain. For the proper functioning of the brain, fats can't directly act as energy; it either works on ketones or glucose.

As the energy source of the body changes to ketones, there comes an increase in fat burning and a considerable lowering in insulin levels. This allows the fat to burn efficiently and be accessible conveniently. This process stimulates weight loss alongside lower appetite and enhanced energy for mental and physical tasks.

The process in which ketones are produced is known as ketosis. Ketones can be efficiently produced by fasting but it has a drawback that fasting cannot be done for a longer time period. The ketogenic diet is an alternative to fasting and yields the same results as fasting including weight loss etc. without going through fasting at all.

Is keto right for you?

The ketogenic diet plan has tremendous positive effects on people across the globe and has gathered a fan base with strong positive reviews. It is generally considered to be very safe, sound, efficient and easy to adapt but there are a few special cases which do needs extra consideration and attention. These include:

- Individuals suffering from diabetes (individuals taking insulin injections or any other form)
- Individuals having a history of high BP. (those individuals who are taking medications for complaints of high blood pressure etc.)
- Mothers who are breastfeeding.

How to know whether you are in ketosis?

There are numerous ways to test you being in ketosis. These methods include blood samples, breath sample and urine testing. Apart from these testing methods, there are certain physical signs of ketosis which can be felt and seen without the aids of any testing at all. These symptoms include:

- Dry Mouth and Increase in Thirst:
  The lower consumption of electrolytes like salt and not drinking enough water might lead towards a condition in which the mouth becomes dry. To avoid this, it is strictly recommended to enhance water intake as much as you can and also 1-2 cups of

bouillon on daily basis. It is also important to note that you will feel a metallic taste in your mouth.

- More Urination:

As you start consuming keto diet, 'acetoacetate' will end up in your urine which is ketonic compound. It is due to this compound that ketosis can be effectively tested by a urine sample. It also causes a rapid increase in urinating more often during the starting and also leads towards more thirst as explained above.

- Keto breath:

'Keto breath' is a special breath resulted due to acetone as it escapes out while exhaling breath. The smell of the breath due to acetone is usually similar to that of a nail polish remover or at times might be even fruity. This is a temporary effect and it fades away after certain time. This specific smell can also be sensed while exercising in the shape of sweat.

There are numerous other symptoms too which are beneficial in nature and can lead to affirming that you are in ketosis.

- Enhanced Energy:

As soon as your 'keto fever; ends, you will feel a considerable increase in the amount of your physical and mental energy. It leads to either having a feeling of being euphoric or having a much-concentrated approach.

- Lesser Urge to Eat:

This is mainly due to the fact that your body has started using the fats for its energy purposes. Generally, individuals following the keto diet get contented with having a single or two diets and unconsciously pass through intermittent fasting. This is very time and money saving and also boosts weight loss a lot.

CHAPTER2: WHAT ARE THE BENEFITS FOR YOU WHEN YOU GO KETO?

The benefits of the keto diet are almost similar to other diet based on lower carb consumption. The keto diet is more effective and powerful in delivering its benefits which makes it standing out in the rest of the similar diet plans. To simply understand the difference, the keto diet is having powerful positive effects and gives the most benefits to the users as compared to other low-carb diet plans. Some of the famous benefits of keto diet are as follows:

- Weight Loss:

  The weight loss efficiency of the keto diet can be understood by the reason that the body starts utilizing already present fats for fueling purposes. As soon as the insulin levels falls, fat burning gets stimulated. This environment paves the way for considerable fat loss which leads to losing weight without fasting. To support this argument, 20 modern day medical and scientific researches have credited the keto diet being the most efficient plan for weight loss than its competitors.

- Controlled Appetite:

  The keto diet gives you appetite controlling. This is credited to the reason that with immense fat burning, the body gets a considerable quantity of fat to gain energy from and doesn't let you get hungry at all. This argument has been readily proved by medical and scientific studies.

  This appetite controlling can be credited to the effective weight loss process in keto plan. It paves a convenient way to undergo intermittent fasting, propagates the process of weight loss and reverses type-2 diabetes. It also helps a lot in lowering your financial burden due to less hunger.

With lesser hunger and appetite controlling you can easily avoid food and sugar addiction and apart from them totally ignoring unwanted things like bulimia etc. It gives you a certain satisfactory feeling which is a critical segment of the solution. The keto plan allows food to become an ally and energy source rather than making it your enemy.

- **More Energy and Boosting Mental Performance:**

  Ketosis lets a constant supply of energy to the brain the shape of ketones and lets you avoid blood sugar swings. It assists in boosting your mental capabilities like enhancing your concentration & focus level and fades away brain fog. The mental health boosting advantages of the keto diet has made it very popular than its competitors. You can easily feel these advantages while being in the process of ketosis. The reason for all this enhancement of mental capabilities is that in ketosis you get a constant supply of enough energy to your brain in the form of ketones instead of carbs.

- **Effects on Type-2 Diabetes & Blood Sugar Controlling:**

  The keto diet has a tremendous role and benefit in controlling the blood sugar levels and reverses the type-2 diabetes which has been proved both scientifically and medically. The keto diet reduces the harmful impacts of high insulin levels and keeps the blood sugar levels very low which is why it helps in reversing type-2 diabetes so effectively.

  Even that it helps in reversing type-2 diabetes, it can be logically understood that the keto diet lets you prevent yourself from having type-2 diabetes in the first place.

- Betterment in Health Markers:

  With so much scientific and medical research it has been proved that lower carb consumption leads to betterment in important health markers like Blood Pressure level, cholesterol levels and blood sugar levels.

  Metabolic syndrome, type-2 diabetes reversal, waist circumference and weight improvement are linked to these health markers.

- Stomach Betterment:

  The keto diet allows you to have a tremendous betterment in your digestive system. It prevents pains and cramps while also leads to lesser or even not any gas at all inside the stomach. You can experience the benefits related to digestive system in the starting 2-3 days of your diet plan.

- Betterment in Physical Endurance:

  With surplus provision of energy from fat burning, the keto diet provides you with stronger and intense physical endurance and strength. If you go through high level exercising, the energy provided by glucose (carbs) will be consumed in a few hours while the energy due to ketones can remain in your body from weeks to months. This is why you get a strong boost in your physical endurance level.

- Treatment of Epilepsy:

  Since 1920s, the keto diet has been used for treating the patients of epilepsy. This is backed by a lot of medical and scientific findings and researches. In the starting it was only applied at children but recently it has been started to apply on adults and it has shown remarkable results.

The patients of epilepsy halt using any medication or in cases lesser medications after switching to keto without even having a slight fear of having a seizure. Due to this, drug intake lowers and so does their harmful side effects which allow you to strengthen your mental capabilities even more.

- **Additional Benefits:**

    There are many more benefits of the keto diet which can prove to be life changing for numerous people apart from the above-mentioned advantages it offers. Migraine control, controlled BP, fewer acne problems and even assisting in certain mental conditions has been referred to the keto diet. Some of the notable additional benefits of the keto diet are as follows:

    - It benefits in having fewer acne issues.
    - It assists in reversing PCOS.
    - It aids in having fewer heartburns.
    - It helps in having fewer migraine attacks.
    - It assists in the treatment of brain cancer.
    - It lets you have fewer sugar cravings.
    - It is used for treating Alzheimer's disease.
    - It helps in normalizing blood pressure levels.

According to a recent scientific and medical study, the keto diet can be used for treating or even reducing the risk of having cancer. It is recently being subjected for experiment for treating people with Parkinson's disease.

CHAPTER3: FOODS TO EAT

1. Leafy Green foods like spinach etc.
2. Dairy products like cheese, butter etc.
3. Fruits like raspberries etc.

It is critical to understand that for being effectively in ketosis, your carb/100g intake should be low. The process of ketosis is directly linked to lower carb intake and this is the only effective way of achieving it. Carb consumption should not at any cost exceed 50g/day and to be in more effective ketosis, it should be around 20 g/day. The while agenda is simple; 'lower carbs lead to more effective keto diet plan'.

What is recommended for Drinking?

The most preferred and advantageous beverage for keto lovers is water. You can also drink tea or coffee but its nit allowed for you to add sweeteners in it like sugar etc. A small quantity of milk or cream in your tea or coffee is allowed but you can't go for a coffee latte. You can also drink a glass of wine on occasional grounds.

CHAPTER4: FOODS TO AVOID

1. Grains like corn, rice etc.
2. Sugary foods like honey etc.
3. Bread
4. Pasta
5. Potatoes

Those foods which have higher quantity of starch and sugar are not allowed on a keto plan because of their richness in carbohydrates.

It is important to understand that your food should be high in fats with a moderate protein intake. Proteins can be easily converted into blood sugar in the body. For a rough outline, your diet should be having 5% energy from carbs (lower the quantity of carbohydrates, more will be the effectiveness), 15-25% energy should be credited to proteins and the rest of the 75% should be from fat intake.

CHAPTER5: THE COMMON MISTAKES FOR BEGINNERS

Following are some common mistakes which are committed by beginners and can affect your keto diet plan's efficiency.

- Not following the plan properly on regular basis
- Consuming too much proteins
- Not considering planning your meal
- Not consuming the required amount of fats
- Consuming Processed fats
- Sleep deprivation
- Not remaining properly hydrated
- Always comparing your progress with others

CHAPTER6: CAN I WORK OUT ON THE KETO DIET?

The answer is yes! It is commonly thought that carbs are the sole providers of energy to the body and as soon as their consumption drops, you will feel a considerable amount of loss in your energy to perform physical tasks like working out. As mentioned earlier, in ketosis the body changes your energy source from glucose to ketone and thus you get the required amount of energy for physical activities. So, if you are following the keto plan, ignore all the myths and go for your working out session with confidence, we guarantee that you will be even more energetic than non-keto followers.

CHAPTER7: FAQS

As a beginner you will be having a lot of question in your mind before starting your keto plan. We have tried clearing everything regarding the keto diet plan and its working, yet we are answering certain FAQS which are as follows:

- How much weight loss can I lose on a keto diet?

  Weight losing scale is varying from person to person on a keto plan. Generally, in the start you will lose around 1-2kg weight which is actually linked to water weight. After the starting week, usually people lose around 0.5kg fat per week. It is important to note that this rate of weight loss may differ from person to person and younger people might experience a faster rate of weight loss while women aged above 40 might feel a considerable lower rate of weight loss.

  As you achieve your regular body weight, the weight loss process will get a slower pace. If you keep on eating food whenever you're hungry, you will get a stable weight irrespective of being on the keto plan.

- How do I record of my carb intake?

  Most of the time the diets are planned in such a way that your carb intake will be lower than 20 carbs/day without the need to count them. There are different ways to measure your carb intake if it's not notified in your diet plan. These include Chronometer or MyFitnessPal app.

- What to do after achieving my health and weight aims on a keto plan?

  It is preferred that you should keep on following the plan as it is as the moment you stop following it, after sometime you will find yourself from where you started, thus nullifying the purpose of following the plan itself. A little addition of carb might work but for sure will lower the efficiency of the keto plan.

CHAPTER8: MEAL PLAN

Week One 7 Day Keto Menu Plan

Day One

Breakfast:

Coffee with 2 Tablespoons Cream (Heavy)

Scrambled Eggs

Snack

Eggs Stuffed with Avocado & Watercress

Lunch

4 Romaine Lettuce Leaves

Air Fried Chicken

2 slices bacon (cooked)

Snack

24 almonds (raw)

Dinner

3/4 cup Easy Cauliflower Gratin

Caprese Hassel back Chicken

2 Tablespoon Caesar Salad Dressing (sugar-less)

2 cups romaine lettuce (chopped)

Dessert

Chocolate Peanut Butter Cups

Day Two

Breakfast:

Coffee with 2 Tablespoon Cream (heavy)

Tofu with Mushrooms

Snack

Creamy Chicken Breasts

Lunch

2 Tablespoon Caesar Salad Dressing (sugar-less)

2 cups romaine lettuce (chopped)

1 cup leftover chicken (chopped)

Snack

Cheese Casserole

Dinner

Garlic Creamy Beef Steak

Dessert

Crème Brûlée

Day Three

Breakfast:

Coffee with 2 Tablespoon Cream (heavy)

Bacon Veggies Combo

Snack

2 String Cheese

Lunch

3/4 cup Easy Cauliflower Gratin

Creamy Chicken Breasts

Snack

Spinach Quiche

Dinner

1 Tablespoon ranch dressing (sugar-less)

2 cups baby spinach (raw)

Greek Lamb Gyros

Dessert

Flourless Chocolate Brownies

Day Four

Breakfast:

Coffee with 2 Tablespoon Cream (heavy)

Sausage and Spinach Frittata (3-inch square)

Snack

1/2 hass avocado with lite salt and pepper

Lunch

Creamy Chicken Tenders

Snack

Avocado Chips

Dinner

4 Tomato and Feta Meatballs (sundried)

1/2 cup "Anti" Pasta Salad

1 Tablespoon Italian dressing (sugar-less)

Lamb Roast

Dessert

Chocolate Peanut Butter Cups

Day Five

Breakfast:

Coffee with 2 Tablespoon Cream (heavy)

Onion Tofu Scramble

Snack

1 cup bone broth

Lunch

4 Tomato and Feta Meatballs (sundried)

Ham Stuffed Turkey Rolls

Snack

Scallion Cake

Dinner

2 cups romaine lettuce (chopped)

1 cup taco salad style Cuban Pot Roast

2 Tablespoons cream (sour)

Lamb Roast

Dessert

Crème Brûlée

Day Six

Breakfast:

Coffee with 2 Tablespoon Cream (heavy)

Pepperoni Omelet

Snack

24 almonds (raw)

Lunch

2 cups romaine lettuce (chopped)

1 cup taco salad style Cuban Pot Roast

2 Tablespoon cream (sour)

1/4 cup cheddar cheese (shredded)

Optional 1 Tablespoon cilantro (chopped)

Snack

Mixed Nuts

Dinner

1 Tablespoon ranch dressing (sugar-less)

2 cups baby spinach (raw)

Zesty Lamb Chops

Dessert

Flourless Chocolate Brownies

Day Seven

Breakfast:

Coffee with 2 Tablespoon Cream (heavy)

Ham Spinach Ballet

Snack

2 String Cheese

Lunch

4 Tomato and Feta Meatballs (sundried)

Stuffed Whole Chicken

Snack

Asparagus Bites

Dinner

2 cups romaine lettuce (chopped)

1 cup taco salad style Cuban Pot Roast

Mustard Pork Chops

¼ cup cheddar cheese (shredded)

Optional 1 Tablespoon cilantro (chopped)

Dessert

Cream Crepes

Week Two 7 Day Keto Menu Plan

Day 1

Breakfast:

Coffee with 2 Tablespoon Cream (heavy)

2 pieces bacon (cooked)

Sausage Solo

Snack

12 almonds (raw)

Lunch

Creamy Turkey Breast

1 cup Jalapeno Popper Soup

Snack

Broccoli Pops

Dinner

1 Tablespoon ranch dressing (sugar-less)

2 cups baby spinach (raw)

Lamb Roast

Dessert

Nut Porridge

Day 2

Breakfast:

Coffee with 2 Tablespoon Cream (heavy)

Bacon Bok Choy Samba

Snack

1/2 avocado with lite salt and pepper

Lunch

Caprese Hassel back Chicken

Snack

Zucchini Cream Cheese Fries

Dinner

1 Tablespoon ranch dressing (sugar-less)

1 Paprika Chicken Thigh with sauce

2 cups baby spinach (raw)

1/2 cup Cheesy Cauliflower Puree

Dessert

Lemon Mousse

Day 3

Breakfast:

Coffee with 2 Tablespoon Cream (heavy)

Scrambled Eggs

Snack

1/2 avocado with lite salt and pepper

Lunch

Mediterranean Turkey Cutlets

1 Paprika Chicken Thigh with sauce

Snack

Keto Onion Rings

Dinner

2 Tablespoon Italian dressing (sugar-less)

1 cup Jalapeno Popper Soup

2 cups romaine lettuce (chopped)

1 Jalapeno and Cheddar Muffin

Dessert

Chocolate Cheese Cake

Day 4

Breakfast:

Coffee with 2 Tablespoon Cream (heavy)

1 Jalapeno and Cheddar Muffin

Tofu with Mushrooms

Snack

1 cup bone broth

Lunch

Keto Garlic Turkey Breasts

Snack

Eggs Stuffed with Avocado & Watercress

Dinner

2 Tablespoon Italian dressing (sugar-less)

1 cup Jalapeno Popper Soup

2 cups romaine lettuce (chopped)

Lamb Roast

Dessert

Vanilla Yogurt

Day 5

Breakfast:

Coffee with 2 Tablespoon Cream (heavy)

Bacon Veggies Combo

1 Jalapeno and Cheddar Muffin

Lunch

1 Tablespoon Italian dressing (sugar-less)

2 cups baby spinach (raw)

Chili Lime Turkey

Snack

Spinach Quiche

Dinner

2 Tablespoon Italian dressing (sugar-less)

2 cups romaine lettuce (chopped)

Zesty Lamb Chops

Dessert

Chocolate Peanut Butter Cups

Day 6

Breakfast:

Coffee with 2 Tablespoon Cream (heavy)

1 teaspoon butter

Onion Tofu Scramble

Snack

12 almonds (raw)

Lunch

1 Jalapeno and Cheddar Muffin

Salmon Stew

Snack

Cheese Casserole

Dinner

2 Tablespoon Italian dressing (sugar-less)

1 Paprika Chicken Thigh with sauce

2 cups romaine lettuce (chopped)

Mustard Pork Chops

Dessert

Crème Brûlée

Day 7

Breakfast:

Coffee with 2 Tablespoon Cream (heavy)

Pepperoni Omelet

Snack

½ avocado with lite salt and pepper

Lunch

3 Meatballs alla Parmigiana

Snack

Avocado Chips

Dinner

2 Tablespoon Italian dressing (sugar-less)

1 Paprika Chicken Thigh with sauce

2 cups romaine lettuce (chopped)

Paprika Shrimp

Dessert

Lindt 90% Chocolate (2 squares)

Week Three 7 Day Keto Menu Plan

Day 1

Breakfast:

Ham Spinach Ballet

2 Cream Cheese Pancakes

Snack

12 almonds (raw)

Lunch

1 Tablespoon mayonnaise

2 Cream Cheese Pancakes

2 slices deli cheddar cheese

Ketogenic Butter Fish

Snack

Scallion Cake

Dinner

Mustard Pork Chops

3/4 cup Cheesy Chipotle Cauliflower

Dessert

Flourless Chocolate Brownies

Day 2

Breakfast

Sausage Solo

1 serving Ham and Cheese Frittata

Snack

2 string cheese

Lunch

Shrimp Magic

Snack

Mixed Nuts

Dinner

Mexican Taco Casserole

1 3/4 cup Sausage, squash and Kale soup

Dessert

Cream Crepes

Day 3

Breakfast

Coffee with 2 Tablespoon Cream (heavy)

Bacon Bok Choy Samba

Snack

½ avocado with lite salt and pepper

Lunch

2 Tablespoon Italian dressing (sugar-less)

2 cups romaine lettuce (chopped)

Sweet and Sour Fish

Snack

Asparagus Bites

Dinner

Pork Carnitas

3/4 cup Chipotle Cauliflower (cheesy)

Dessert

Nut Porridge

Day 4

Breakfast

Coffee with 2 Tablespoon Cream (heavy)

Scrambled Eggs

2 pieces bacon (cooked)

Snack

12 almonds (raw)

Lunch

Buttered Scallops

Snack

Broccoli Pops

Dinner

2 Tablespoon Italian dressing (sugar-less)

2 cups romaine lettuce (chopped)

Jamaican Jerk Pork Roast

Dessert

Lemon Mousse

Day 5

Breakfast

Coffee with 2 Tablespoon Cream (heavy)

2 pieces bacon (cooked)

Tofu with Mushrooms

Snack

1 serving Ham and Cheese Frittata

Lunch

Buffalo Fish

Snack

Zucchini Cream Cheese Fries

Dinner

2 Enchilada Meatballs (green)

Crock Pot Beef Fajitas

Dessert

1 Raspberry Cheesecake Bar

Day 6

Breakfast

Coffee with 2 Tablespoon Cream (heavy)

Bacon Veggies Combo

2 pieces bacon (cooked)

Snack

2 string cheese

Lunch

Cod: Battle of Herbs

Snack

Keto Onion Rings

Dinner

1 3/4 cup Sausage, squash and Kale soup

2 Tablespoon Italian dressing (sugar-less)

Bacon Swiss Pork Chops

Dessert

Chocolate Cheese Cake

Day 7

Breakfast

Coffee with 2 Tablespoon Cream (heavy)

2 pieces bacon (cooked)

2 Cream Cheese Pancakes

Snack

1 string cheese

Lunch

2 Enchilada Meatballs (green)

Garlic Creamy Beef Steak

Snack

Keto Onion Rings

Dinner

1/2 cup serving Broccoli Slaw

Ketogenic Beef Sirloin Steak

Dessert

Vanilla Yogurt

CHAPTER9: BREAKFAST RECIPES

Scrambled Eggs

Preparation Time: 5 minutes
Cooking Time: 8 minutes
Servings: 2
Ingredients:

- 4 eggs
- 1 tablespoon butter
- 1 tablespoon milk
- Salt and freshly ground black pepper, to taste

Method:

1. Mix together eggs, milk, salt and black pepper in a medium bowl.
2. Put butter in a pan and heat over medium-low heat.
3. Slowly add the whisked eggs mixture and continuously stir for about 4 minutes.
4. Dish out the scrambled eggs in a serving plate.

Nutritional Value:

- *Calories 151*
- *Total Fat 11.6 g*
- *Saturated Fat 4.6 g*
- *Cholesterol 335 mg*
- *Total Carbs 0.7 g*
- *Sugar 0.7 g*
- *Fiber 0 g*
- *Sodium 144 mg*
- *Potassium 119 mg*
- *Protein 11.1 g*

Tofu with Mushrooms

Preparation Time: 5 minutes
Cooking Time: 25 minutes
Servings: 6
Ingredients:

- 2 cups fresh mushrooms, chopped finely
- 8 tablespoons Parmesan cheese, shredded
- 2 blocks tofu, pressed and cubed into 1-inch pieces
- 8 tablespoons butter
- Salt and freshly ground black pepper, to taste

Method:

1. Mix together tofu, salt and black pepper in a bowl.
2. Put butter in a pan and heat over medium-low heat.
3. Add the seasoned tofu and cook for about 5 minutes.
4. Stir in the Parmesan cheese and mushrooms and cook for about 4 minutes, occasionally stirring.
5. Dish out in a serving plate and serve hot.

Nutritional Value:

- *Calories 211*
- *Total Fat 18.5 g*
- *Saturated Fat 11.5 g*
- *Cholesterol 51 mg*
- *Total Carbs 2 g*
- *Sugar 0.5 g*
- *Fiber 0.4 g*
- *Sodium 346 mg*
- *Potassium 93 mg*
- *Protein 11.5 g*

Bacon Veggies Combo

Preparation Time: 5 minutes
Cooking Time: 25 minutes
Servings: 4
Ingredients:

- 4 bacon slices
- 1 green bell pepper, seeded and chopped
- ½ cup Parmesan Cheese
- 2 scallions, chopped
- 1 tablespoon avocado mayonnaise

Method:

1. Preheat the oven to 375 degrees F and grease a baking dish with cooking spray.
2. Arrange the baking dish with bacon slices and top with bell peppers, avocado mayonnaise, Parmesan Cheese and scallions.
3. Bake for 25 minutes and serve immediately.

Nutritional Value:

- *Calories 197*
- *Total Fat 13.8 g*
- *Saturated Fat 5.8 g*
- *Cholesterol 37 mg*
- *Total Carbs 4.7 g*
- *Sugar 1.9 g*
- *Fiber 0.6 g*
- *Sodium 662 mg*
- *Potassium 184 mg*
- *Protein 14.3 g*

Onion Tofu Scramble

Preparation Time: 8 minutes
Cooking Time: 12 minutes
Servings: 4

Ingredients:

- 2 blocks tofu, pressed and cubed into 1 inch pieces
- 4 tablespoons butter
- 1 cup cheddar cheese, grated
- 2 medium onions, sliced
- Salt and freshly ground black pepper, to taste

Method:

1. Mix together tofu, salt and black pepper in a bowl.
2. Put butter in a pan and heat over medium-low heat.
3. Add onions and cook for about 3 minutes.
4. Add tofu mixture and cook for about 2 minutes.
5. Add cheddar cheese and cover the pan with lid.
6. Cook for about 5 minutes on low heat and dish out in a bowl.

Nutritional Value:

- *Calories 184*
- *Total Fat 12.7 g*
- *Saturated Fat 7.3 g*
- *Cholesterol 35 mg*
- *Total Carbs 6.3 g*
- *Sugar 2.7 g*
- *Fiber 1.6 g*
- *Sodium 222 mg*
- *Potassium 174 mg*
- *Protein 12.2 g*

Pepperoni Omelet

Preparation Time: 5 minutes
Cooking Time: 30 minutes
Servings: 8
Ingredients:

- 30 pepperoni slices
- 8 tablespoons cream
- 4 tablespoons butter
- 12 eggs
- Salt and freshly ground black pepper, to taste

Method:

1. Whisk together the eggs and the remaining ingredients in a bowl.
2. Put butter in a pan and heat over medium-low heat.
3. Add the egg mixture and cook for about 2 minutes.
4. Flip the sides and cook for another 2 minutes.
5. Dish out in a serving plate and serve immediately.

Nutritional Value:

- *Calories 141*
- *Total Fat 11.3 g*
- *Saturated Fat 3.8 g*
- *Cholesterol 181 mg*
- *Total Carbs 0.6 g*
- *Sugar 0.5 g*
- *Fiber 0 g*
- *Sodium 334 mg*
- *Potassium 103 mg*
- *Protein 8.9 g*

Ham Spinach Ballet

Preparation Time: 5 minutes
Cooking Time: 30 minutes
Servings: 8
Ingredients:

- 3 pounds fresh baby spinach
- ½ cup cream
- 28-ounce ham, sliced
- 4 tablespoons butter, melted
- Salt and freshly ground black pepper, to taste

Method:

1. Preheat the oven to 360 degrees F and grease 8 ramekins with butter.
2. Put butter in a pan and heat over medium-low heat.
3. Add spinach and cook for about 3 minutes.
4. Drain the liquid from the spinach completely and add cooked spinach.
5. Top with cream, ham slices, salt and black pepper and bake for about 25 minutes.
6. Dish out in a large serving bowl and serve hot.

Nutritional Value:

- *Calories 188*
- *Total Fat 12.5 g*
- *Saturated Fat 4.4 g*
- *Cholesterol 53 mg*
- *Total Carbs 4.9 g*
- *Sugar 0.3 g*
- *Fiber 2 g*
- *Sodium 1098 mg*
- *Potassium 484 mg*
- *Protein 14.6 g*

Sausage Solo

Preparation Time: 5 minutes
Cooking Time: 30 minutes
Servings: 2
Ingredients:

- 2 cooked sausages, sliced
- 2 eggs
- 1 tablespoon butter
- ¼ cup cream
- ¼ cup mozzarella cheese, grated

Method:

1. Preheat the oven to 360 degrees F and grease 2 ramekins with butter.
2. Mix together eggs and cream in a bowl and beat well.
3. Put the egg mixture into ramekins and top evenly with cheese and sausage slices.
4. Transfer the ramekins in the oven and cook for about 20 minutes.
5. Dish out and serve immediately.

Nutritional Value:

- *Calories 180*
- *Total Fat 12.7 g*
- *Saturated Fat 4.7 g*
- *Cholesterol 264 mg*
- *Total Carbs 3.9 g*
- *Sugar 1.3 g*
- *Fiber 0.1 g*
- *Sodium 251 mg*
- *Potassium 142 mg*
- *Protein 12.4 g*

Bacon Bok Choy Samba

Preparation Time: 5 minutes
Cooking Time: 15 minutes
Servings: 6
Ingredients:

- 4 bacon slices
- 2 tablespoons olive oil
- 8 tablespoons cream
- 8 bok choy, sliced
- 1 cup Parmesan cheese, grated
- Salt and freshly ground black pepper, to taste

Method:

1. Season bok choy with salt and black pepper.
2. Put oil in a skillet and heat on medium-high heat.
3. Add bacon slices and sauté for about 5 minutes.
4. Stir in cream and bok choy and sauté for about 6 minutes.
5. Top with Parmesan cheese and cook for 4 minutes on low heat.
6. Dish out in a serving platter and serve.

Nutritional Value:

- *Calories 112*
- *Total Fat 4.9 g*
- *Saturated Fat 1.9 g*
- *Cholesterol 10 mg*
- *Total Carbs 1.9 g*
- *Sugar 0.8 g*
- *Fiber 0.4 g*
- *Sodium 355 mg*
- *Potassium 101 mg*
- *Protein 3 g*

CHAPTER 10: APPETIZERS AND SNACKS RECIPES

Eggs Stuffed with Avocado & Watercress

Preparation Time: 10 minutes
Cooking Time: 5 minutes
Servings: 3
Ingredients:

- ½ medium ripe avocado, peeled, pitted and chopped
- ¼ tablespoon fresh lemon juice
- 3 organic eggs, boiled, peeled and cut in half lengthwise
- ¼ cup fresh watercress, trimmed
- Salt, to taste

Method:

1. Place a steamer basket at the bottom of the pressure cooker and pour water.
2. Put the watercress on the trivet and lock the lid.
3. Cook for about 3 minutes at high pressure.
4. Quickly release the pressure and completely drain the watercress.
5. Remove the egg yolks and transfer into a bowl.
6. Add avocado, watercress, lemon juice and salt and mash completely with a fork.
7. Arrange the egg whites in a serving plate and stuff the egg whites with watercress mixture.

Nutritional Value:

- *Calories 132*
- *Total Fat 10.9 g*
- *Saturated Fat 2.7 g*
- *Cholesterol 164 mg*
- *Total Carbs 3.3 g*
- *Sugar 0.5 g*
- *Fiber 2.3 g*
- *Sodium 65 mg*
- *Potassium 226 mg*
- *Protein 6.3 g*

Spinach Quiche

Preparation Time: 10 minutes
Cooking Time: 35 minutes
Servings: 6
Ingredients:

- 1 (10-ounce) package frozen spinach, thawed
- 1 tablespoon butter, melted
- 5 organic eggs, beaten
- 3 cups Monterey Jack cheese, shredded
- Salt and freshly ground black pepper, to taste

Method:

1. Preheat the oven to 350 degrees F and lightly grease a 9-inch pie dish.
2. Put butter in a large skillet and heat on medium-low heat.
3. Add spinach and cook for about 3 minutes and set aside.
4. Mix together eggs, Monterey Jack cheese, cooked spinach, salt and black pepper in a bowl.
5. Put the mixture into prepared pie dish and bake for about 30 minutes.
6. Remove from the oven and cut into equal sized wedges to serve.

Nutritional Value:

- *Calories 349*
- *Total Fat 27.8 g*
- *Saturated Fat 14.8 g*
- *Cholesterol 229 mg*
- *Total Carbs 3.2 g*
- *Sugar 1.3 g*
- *Fiber 1.3 g*
- *Sodium 532 mg*
- *Potassium 466 mg*
- *Protein 23 g*

Cheese Casserole

Preparation Time: 15 minutes
Cooking Time: 22 minutes
Servings: 6
Ingredients:

- 10-ounce parmesan, shredded
- 16-ounce marinara sauce
- 2 tablespoons olive oil
- 2 pounds sausage scramble
- 16-ounce mozzarella cheese, shredded

Method:

1. Preheat the oven to 375 degrees F and grease a baking dish with the olive oil.
2. Place half of the sausage scramble in the baking dish.
3. Spread half of the marinara over the sausage scramble.
4. Top with half of the mozzarella and Parmesan cheese.
5. Layer with the remaining half of the sausage scramble and spread the remaining half of Parmesan and mozzarella cheese.
6. Top with rest of the marinara sauce and bake in the oven for 22 minutes.
7. Dish out and serve hot.

Nutritional Value:

- *Calories 521*
- *Total Fat 38.8 g*
- *Saturated Fat 12.8 g*
- *Cholesterol 136 mg*
- *Total Carbs 6 g*
- *Sugar 5.4 g*
- *Fiber 0 g*
- *Sodium 201 mg*
- *Potassium 506 mg*
- *Protein 35.4 g*

Avocado Chips

Preparation Time: 10 minutes
Cooking Time: 10 minutes
Servings: 2
Ingredients:

- 2 raw avocados, peeled and sliced in chips form
- 2 tablespoons butter
- Salt and freshly ground pepper, to taste

Method:

1. Preheat the oven to 355 degrees F and grease a baking dish with cooking spray.
2. Top with butter and avocado slices evenly and place in oven.
3. Bake for about 10 minutes and sprinkle with salt and black pepper.

Nutritional Value:

- *Calories 391*
- *Total Fat 38.2 g*
- *Saturated Fat 11 g*
- *Cholesterol 31 mg*
- *Total Carbs 15 g*
- *Sugar 0.5 g*
- *Fiber 11.8 g*
- *Sodium 96 mg*
- *Potassium 881 mg*
- *Protein 3.5 g*

Scallion Cake

Preparation Time: 10 minutes
Cooking Time: 20 minutes
Servings: 4
Ingredients:

- ¼ cup flax seeds meal
- ½ cup Parmesan cheese, grated finely
- ½ teaspoon baking powder
- ½ cup low-fat cottage cheese
- 1/3 cup scallion, sliced thinly
- ½ cup almond meal
- ¼ cup nutritional yeast flakes
- 6 organic eggs, beaten
- ½ cup raw hemp seeds
- Salt, to taste

Method:

1. Preheat the oven to 375 degrees F and grease 4 ramekins with oil.
2. Mix together hemp seeds, baking powder, almond meal, flax seeds meal and salt in a large bowl.
3. Mix eggs and cottage cheese in another bowl and put this mixture into almond meal mixture.
4. Mix until well combined and gently fold in scallion.
5. Transfer the mixture evenly into ramekins evenly and bake for about 20 minutes.

Nutritional Value:

- *Calories 306*
- *Total Fat 19.7 g*
- *Saturated Fat 4.7 g*
- *Cholesterol 0 mg*
- *Total Carbs 10.7 g*
- *Sugar 1.3 g*
- *Fiber 4.2 g*
- *Sodium 398 mg*

- *Potassium 131 mg*
- *Protein 23.5 g*

Mixed Nuts

Preparation Time: 5 minutes
Cooking Time: 14 minutes
Servings: 5
Ingredients:

- 1 cup raw almonds
- 1 tablespoon butter, melted
- 1 cup raw peanuts
- ½ cup raw cashew nuts
- Salt, to taste

Method:

1. Preheat the oven at 320 degrees F and grease a baking dish with cooking spray.
2. Place the nuts in a baking dish and transfer in the oven.
3. Bake for about 10 minutes, tossing twice in between.
4. Remove the nuts from the oven and transfer into a bowl.
5. Add salt and melted butter and toss to coat well.
6. Return the nuts mixture into the oven and bake for about 5 minutes.

Nutritional Value:

- *Calories 189*
- *Total Fat 16.5 g*
- *Saturated Fat 2.2 g*
- *Cholesterol 0 mg*
- *Total Carbs 6.6 g*
- *Sugar 1.3 g*
- *Fiber 2.6 g*
- *Sodium 19 mg*
- *Potassium 211 mg*
- *Protein 6.8 g*

Asparagus Bites

Preparation Time: 15 minutes
Cooking Time: 10 minutes
Servings: 6

Ingredients:

- 1 cup desiccated coconut
- 2 cups asparagus
- 1 cup feta cheese

Method:

1. Preheat the oven to 390 degrees F and grease a baking dish.
2. Place the coconut in a shallow dish and coat asparagus with coconut evenly.
3. Place coated asparagus in the oven and top with cheese.
4. Bake for about 10 minutes and serve.

Nutritional Value:

- *Calories 135*
- *Total Fat 10.3 g*
- *Saturated Fat 7.7 g*
- *Cholesterol 33 mg*
- *Total Carbs 5 g*
- *Sugar 3.1 g*
- *Fiber 2 g*
- *Sodium 421 mg*
- *Potassium 178 mg*
- *Protein 7 g*

Broccoli Pops

Preparation Time: 15 minutes
Cooking Time: 12 minutes
Servings: 6
Ingredients:

- 3 eggs, beaten
- 1/3 cup Parmesan cheese, grated
- 3 cups broccoli florets
- 2 cups cheddar cheese, grated
- 1 tablespoon olive oil
- Salt and freshly ground black pepper, to taste

Method:

1. Put broccoli in a food processor and pulse till finely crumbed.
2. Add broccoli and remaining ingredients in a large bowl and mix until well combined.
3. Make small equal-sized balls from mixture.
4. Arrange balls in a baking sheet and refrigerate for at least 30 minutes.
5. Preheat the oven to 350 degrees F and grease a baking dish with olive oil.
6. Place balls in the baking dish and transfer into oven.
7. Bake for about 12 minutes and dish out.

Nutritional Value:

- Calories 162
- Total Fat 12.4 g
- Saturated Fat 7.6 g
- Cholesterol 69 mg
- Total Carbs 1.9 g
- Sugar 0.5 g
- Fiber 0.5 g
- Sodium 263 mg
- Potassium 100 mg
- Protein 11.2 g

Zucchini Cream Cheese Fries

Preparation Time: 10 minutes
Cooking Time: 20 minutes
Servings: 4
Ingredients:

- 1 cup cream cheese
- 1-pound zucchini, sliced into 2 ½-inch sticks
- 2 tablespoons olive oil
- Salt, to taste

Method:

1. Place zucchini in a colander and sprinkle with salt.
2. Add cream cheese and keep aside for about 10 minutes.
3. Preheat the oven to 390 degrees F and grease a baking dish with olive oil.
4. Place zucchini in the baking dish and transfer into oven.
5. Bake for about 10 minutes and dish out.

Nutritional Value:

- *Calories 374*
- *Total Fat 36.6 g*
- *Saturated Fat 18.4 g*
- *Cholesterol 85 mg*
- *Total Carbs 7.1 g*
- *Sugar 2.8 g*
- *Fiber 1.7 g*
- *Sodium 294 mg*
- *Potassium 488 mg*
- *Protein 7.7 g*

Keto Onion Rings

Preparation Time: 10 minutes
Cooking Time: 10 minutes
Servings: 4
Ingredients:

- 2 large onions, cut into ¼ inch slices
- 2 teaspoons baking powder
- Salt, to taste
- 2 cups cream cheese
- 2 eggs

Method:

1. Preheat the Air fryer to 360 degrees F and separate the onion slices into rings.
2. Mix together baking powder and salt in a shallow dish.
3. Whisk together egg and cream cheese in another shallow dish.
4. Dredge the onion rings into baking powder mixture and dip into egg mixture.
5. Place the onion rings in the air fryer and cook for about 10 minutes.

Nutritional Value:

- *Calories 266*
- *Total Fat 22.5 g*
- *Saturated Fat 13.4 g*
- *Cholesterol 146 mg*
- *Total Carbs 9.9 g*
- *Sugar 3.5 g*
- *Fiber 1.7 g*
- *Sodium 285 mg*
- *Potassium 461 mg*
- *Protein 8 g*

CHAPTER-11: BEEF, PORK AND LAMB RECIPES

Garlic Creamy Beef Steak

Preparation Time: 1 hour
Cooking Time: 30 minutes
Servings: 6
Ingredients:

- 4 garlic cloves, minced
- ½ cup butter
- 2 pounds beef top sirloin steaks
- 1½ cup cream
- Salt and freshly ground black pepper, to taste

Method:

1. Rub the beef sirloin steaks with garlic, salt and black pepper.
2. Marinate the beef with butter and cream and keep aside for 1 hour.
3. Preheat the grill and transfer the steaks on it.
4. Grill for about 15 minutes on each side and serve hot.

Nutritional Value:

- *Calories 353*
- *Total Fat 24.1 g*
- *Saturated Fat 14.5 g*
- *Cholesterol 113 mg*
- *Total Carbs 3.9 g*
- *Sugar 1.2 g*
- *Fiber 0 g*
- *Sodium 298 mg*
- *Potassium 35 mg*
- *Protein 31.8 g*

Ketogenic Beef Sirloin Steak

Preparation Time: 5 minutes
Cooking Time: 30 minutes
Servings: 3
Ingredients:

- ½ teaspoon garlic powder
- 3 tablespoons butter
- 1-pound beef top sirloin steaks
- 1 garlic clove, minced
- Salt and freshly ground black pepper, to taste

Method:

1. Heat butter and add beef sirloin steaks in a large grill pan.
2. Brown the steaks on both sides by cooking for about 2 minutes on each side.
3. Add garlic powder, garlic clove, salt and black pepper and cook for about 14 minutes on each side on medium-high heat.
4. Dish out the steaks in a serving platter and serve.

Nutritional Value:

- *Calories 246*
- *Total Fat 13.1 g*
- *Saturated Fat 7.6 g*
- *Cholesterol 81 mg*
- *Total Carbs 2 g*
- *Sugar 0.1 g*
- *Fiber 0.1 g*
- *Sodium 224 mg*
- *Potassium 11 mg*
- *Protein 31.3 g*

Bacon Swiss Pork Chops

Preparation Time: 5 minutes
Cooking Time: 20 minutes
Servings: 4
Ingredients:

- 4 pork chops, bone-in
- ½ cup Swiss cheese, shredded
- 6 bacon strips, cut in half
- 1 tablespoon butter
- Salt and freshly ground black pepper, to taste

Method:

1. Season the pork chops generously with salt and black pepper.
2. Put butter in the skillet and heat on medium-low heat.
3. Add pork chops and cook for about 6 minutes.
4. Add bacon strips and cook for about 8 minutes.
5. Top with Swiss cheese and cook for about 5 minutes on low heat.
6. Remove from heat and dish out.

Nutritional Value:

- *Calories 483*
- *Total Fat 40 g*
- *Saturated Fat 16.2 g*
- *Cholesterol 89 mg*
- *Total Carbs 0.7 g*
- *Sugar 0.2 g*
- *Fiber 0 g*
- *Sodium 552 mg*
- *Potassium 286 mg*
- *Protein 27.7 g*

Crock Pot Beef Fajitas

Preparation Time: 5 minutes
Cooking Time: 20 minutes
Servings: 4
Ingredients:

- 1 bell pepper, sliced
- 1 tablespoon butter
- 1-pound beef, sliced
- 1 onion, sliced
- 1 tablespoon fajita seasoning

Method:

1. Put the butter in the bottom of the crock pot and add onions, bell pepper, fajita seasoning and beef.
2. Set the crock pot on low and cook for about 9 hours.
3. Dish out the delicious beef fajitas and serve hot.

Nutritional Value:

- *Calories 353*
- *Total Fat 13.4 g*
- *Saturated Fat 6 g*
- *Cholesterol 145 mg*
- *Total Carbs 8.5 g*
- *Sugar 3.6 g*
- *Fiber 1.3 g*
- *Sodium 304 mg*
- *Potassium 738 mg*
- *Protein 46.7 g*

Jamaican Jerk Pork Roast

Preparation Time: 10 minutes
Cooking Time: 25 minutes
Servings: 3
Ingredients:

- 1-pound pork shoulder
- 1 tablespoon butter
- 1/8 cup Jamaican jerk spice blend
- 1/8 cup beef broth

Method:

1. Season the pork with Jamaican jerk spice blend.
2. Heat the butter in the pot and add seasoned pork.
3. Cook for about 5 minutes and add beef broth.
4. Cover the lid and cook for about 20 minutes on low heat.
5. Dish out in a serving platter and serve hot.

Nutritional Value:

- *Calories 477*
- *Total Fat 36.2 g*
- *Saturated Fat 14.3 g*
- *Cholesterol 146 mg*
- *Total Carbs 0 g*
- *Sugar 0 g*
- *Fiber 0 g*
- *Sodium 162 mg*
- *Potassium 507 mg*
- *Protein 35.4 g*

Pork Carnitas

Preparation Time: 10 minutes
Cooking Time: 12 minutes
Servings: 3
Ingredients:

- 1 orange, juiced
- 1 tablespoon butter
- 1-pound pork shoulder, bone-in
- ½ teaspoon garlic powder
- Salt and freshly ground black pepper, to taste

Directions:

1. Season the pork with salt and black pepper.
2. Put butter in the pressure cooker and add garlic powder.
3. Sauté for 1 minute and add seasoned pork.
4. Sauté for 3 minutes and pour orange juice.
5. Lock the lid and cook at high pressure for about 8 minutes.
6. Naturally release the pressure and dish out.

Nutritional Value:

- *Calories 506*
- *Total Fat 36.3 g*
- *Saturated Fat 14.3 g*
- *Cholesterol 146 mg*
- *Total carbs 7.6 g*
- *Sugar 5.8 g*
- *Fiber 1.5 g*
- *Sodium 130 mg*
- *Potassium 615 mg*
- *Protein 35.9 g*

Mexican Taco Casserole

Preparation Time: 10 minutes
Cooking Time: 25 minutes
Servings: 3
Ingredients:

- ½ cup cottage cheese
- ½ cup cheddar cheese, shredded
- 1-pound ground beef
- 1 tablespoon taco seasoning
- ½ cup salsa

Directions:

1. Mix together the taco seasoning and ground beef in a bowl.
2. Stir in the cottage cheese, salsa and cheddar cheese.
3. Preheat the oven to 425°F and grease a baking dish.
4. Put the ground beef mixture in the baking dish and top with cheese mixture.
5. Bake for about 25 minutes and serve warm.

Nutritional Value:

- *Calories 409*
- *Total Fat 16.5 g*
- *Saturated Fat 8 g*
- *Cholesterol 158 mg*
- *Total Carbs 5.7 g*
- *Sugar 1.9 g*
- *Fiber 0.6 g*
- *Sodium 769 mg*
- *Potassium 792 mg*
- *Protein 56.4 g*

Mustard Pork Chops

Preparation Time: 10 minutes
Cooking Time: 30 minutes
Servings: 4
Ingredients:

- 2 tablespoons Dijon mustard
- 2 tablespoons butter
- 4 pork chops
- 1 tablespoon fresh rosemary, coarsely chopped
- Salt and freshly ground black pepper, to taste

Method:

1. Marinate the pork chops with Dijon mustard, fresh rosemary, salt and black pepper for about 3 hours.
2. Put the butter and marinated pork chops in a non-stick skillet and cover the lid.
3. Cook for about 30 minutes on medium-low heat.
4. Dish out when completely cooked and serve hot.

Nutritional Value:

- *Calories 315*
- *Total Fat 26.1 g*
- *Saturated Fat 11.2 g*
- *Cholesterol 84 mg*
- *Total Carbs 1 g*
- *Sugar 0.1 g*
- *Fiber 0.6 g*
- *Sodium 186 mg*
- *Potassium 296 mg*
- *Protein 18.4 g*

Zesty Lamb Chops

Preparation Time: 10 minutes
Cooking Time: 45 minutes
Servings: 4
Ingredients:

- 3 tablespoons lemon juice
- 4 tablespoons butter
- 4 lamb chops, bone-in
- 1 cup picante sauce
- 2 tablespoons low-carb flour mix

Method:

1. Coat the chops with flour.
2. Mix picante sauce and orange in a bowl.
3. Heat oil in the instant pot and add the chops.
4. Close the lid and press the meat/stew setting.
5. Set the timer for 35 minutes and cook at high pressure.
6. Release the pressure naturally for 10 minutes.
7. Dish out and serve hot.

Nutritional Value:

- *Calories 284*
- *Total Fat 19.5 g*
- *Saturated Fat 9.7 g*
- *Cholesterol 107 mg*
- *Total Carbs 1 g*
- *Sugar 0.3 g*
- *Fiber 0.4 g*
- *Sodium 150 mg*
- *Potassium 302 mg*
- *Protein 24.8 g*

Lamb Roast

Preparation Time: 10 minutes
Cooking Time: 1 hour 25 minutes
Servings: 6

Ingredients:

- 1 cup onion soup
- 2 pounds lamb roasted Wegman's
- 1 cups beef broth
- Salt and freshly ground black pepper, to taste

Method:

1. Put the lamb roast in the Instant Pot and add beef broth, onion soup, salt and black pepper.
2. Lock the lid and set the pot to "Manual" at "High Pressure" for about 50 minutes.
3. Release the pressure naturally for about 15 minutes and dish out.

Nutritional Value:

- *Calories 349*
- *Total Fat 18.8 g*
- *Saturated Fat 0.2 g*
- *Cholesterol 122 mg*
- *Total Carbs 2.9 g*
- *Sugar 1.2 g*
- *Fiber 0.3 g*
- *Sodium 480 mg*
- *Potassium 57 mg*
- *Protein 39.9 g*

Keto Lamb Minced Meat

Preparation Time: 10 minutes
Cooking Time: 20 minutes
Servings: 4

Ingredients:

- 1-pound ground lamb meat
- 2 tablespoons butter
- 1 cup onions, chopped
- ½ teaspoon turmeric powder
- 1 teaspoon salt
- ½ teaspoon cayenne pepper
- 1 tablespoon garlic, minced
- 1 tablespoon ginger, minced
- ½ teaspoon ground coriander
- ½ teaspoon cumin powder

Method:

1. Put the butter in a pot and add garlic, ginger and onions.
2. Sauté for about 3 minutes and add ground meat and all the spices.
3. Cover the lid and cook for about 20 minutes on medium-high heat.
4. Dish out in a large serving bowl.

Nutritional Value:

- *Calories 304*
- *Total Fat 21.1 g*
- *Saturated Fat 10.7 g*
- *Cholesterol 96 mg*
- *Total Carbs 4.8 g*
- *Sugar 1.3 g*
- *Fiber 1 g*
- *Sodium 705 mg*
- *Potassium 87 mg*
- *Protein 21.8 g*

Greek Lamb Gyros

Preparation Time: 10 minutes
Cooking Time: 15 minutes
Servings: 4
Ingredients:

- 1-pound lamb meat, ground
- 4 garlic cloves
- 1 teaspoon rosemary
- ¾ teaspoons salt
- ¼ teaspoon black pepper
- ½ small onion, chopped
- 1 teaspoon dried oregano
- 1 teaspoon ground marjoram
- ¾ cup water

Method:

1. Put onions, rosemary, garlic, marjoram, salt and black pepper in a food processor and process until well combined.
2. Add ground lamb meat and process again.
3. Press Meat mixture into the Loaf Pan until compact and very tight.
4. Tightly cover with tin foil and poke some holes in the foil.
5. Preheat the oven to 400 degrees F and transfer the loaf pan in the oven.
6. Bake for about 25 minutes and dish out.

Nutritional Value:

- *Calories 242*
- *Total Fat 15.2 g*
- *Saturated Fat 7.1 g*
- *Cholesterol 80 mg*
- *Total Carbs 2.4 g*
- *Sugar 0.4 g*
- *Fiber 0.6 g*
- *Sodium 521 mg*
- *Potassium 38 mg*

- *Protein 21.4 g*

CHAPTER 11: POULTRY RECIPES

Air Fried Chicken

Preparation Time: 10 minutes
Cooking Time: 10 minutes
Servings: 4
Ingredients:

- 2 tablespoons olive oil
- Salt and freshly ground black pepper, to taste
- 8 skinless, boneless chicken tenderloins
- 1 teaspoon turmeric powder
- 2 eggs

Method:

1. Preheat the air fryer to 355°F and coat the basket with olive oil.
2. Whisk together eggs and dip the chicken tenderloins in it.
3. Mix together salt, black pepper and turmeric powder in a bowl and dredge the chicken in it.
4. Transfer the chicken tenderloins in the fryer basket and cook for about 10 minutes.
5. Dish out and serve with dip of your choice.

Nutritional Value:

- *Calories 342*
- *Total Fat 14.9 g*
- *Saturated Fat 4.4 g*
- *Cholesterol 130 mg*
- *Total Carbs 0.4 g*
- *Sugar 0 g*
- *Fiber 0.1 g*
- *Sodium 80 mg*
- *Potassium 14 mg*

Creamy Chicken Breasts

Preparation Time: 10 minutes
Cooking Time: 15 minutes
Servings: 4
Ingredients:

- 1 small onion
- 2 tablespoons butter
- 1-pound chicken breasts
- ½ cup sour cream
- Salt, to taste

Method:

1. Season the chicken breasts generously with salt and keep aside.
2. Heat butter in a skillet on medium-low heat and add onions.
3. Sauté for 3 minutes and add chicken breasts.
4. Cover the lid and cook for about 10 minutes.
5. Stir in the sour cream and cook for about 4 minutes.
6. Stir gently and dish out to serve.

Nutritional Value:

- *Calories 447*
- *Total Fat 26.9 g*
- *Saturated Fat 12.9 g*
- *Cholesterol 172 mg*
- *Total Carbs 3.8 g*
- *Sugar 1.1 g*
- *Fiber 0.5 g*
- *Sodium 206 mg*
- *Potassium 459 mg*
- *Protein 45.3 g*

Creamy Chicken Tenders

Preparation Time: 5 minutes
Cooking Time: 20 minutes
Servings: 6
Ingredients:

- 4 tablespoons butter
- 1 cup cream
- 2 pounds chicken tenders
- 1 cup feta cheese
- Salt and freshly ground black pepper, to taste

Method:

1. Preheat the oven to 350 degrees F and grease a baking dish with cooking spray.
2. Season chicken tenders with salt and black pepper and keep aside for 10 minutes.
3. Heat butter in a non-stick pan and add chicken tenders.
4. Cook for about 5 minutes on both sides and transfer to the baking dish.
5. Top with feta cheese and cream and bake for about 15 minutes.
6. Dish out and serve hot.

Nutritional Value:

- *Calories 447*
- *Total Fat 26.4 g*
- *Saturated Fat 13.1 g*
- *Cholesterol 185 mg*
- *Total Carbs 2.3 g*
- *Sugar 1.8 g*
- *Fiber 0 g*
- *Sodium 477 mg*
- *Potassium 400 mg*
- *Protein 47.7 g*

Ham Stuffed Turkey Rolls

Preparation Time: 10 minutes
Cooking Time: 20 minutes
Servings: 4
Ingredients:

- 4 ham slices
- 2 tablespoons fresh sage leaves
- 4 (6-ounce) turkey cutlets
- 1 tablespoon butter, melted
- Salt and freshly ground black pepper, to taste

Method:

1. Season the turkey cutlets with salt and black pepper.
2. Roll the turkey cutlets and wrap each one tightly with ham slices.
3. Coat each roll with butter and place the sage leaves evenly over each cutlet.
4. Heat a non-stick pan and cook for about 10 minutes on each side.
5. Dish out and serve immediately.

Nutritional Value:

- *Calories 467*
- *Total Fat 24.8 g*
- *Saturated Fat 10 g*
- *Cholesterol 218 mg*
- *Total Carbs 1.7 g*
- *Sugar 0 g*
- *Fiber 0.8 g*
- *Sodium 534 mg*
- *Potassium 645 mg*
- *Protein 56 g*

Stuffed Whole Chicken

Preparation Time: 10 minutes
Cooking Time: 8 hours
Servings: 6
Ingredients:

- 4 whole garlic cloves, peeled
- 1 cup mozzarella cheese
- 1 (2-pound) whole chicken, cleaned, pat dried
- 2 tablespoons fresh lemon juice
- Salt and freshly ground black pepper, to taste

Method:

1. Stuff the chicken cavity with mozzarella cheese and garlic cloves and season the chicken with salt and black pepper.
2. Transfer the chicken in the crock pot and drizzle lemon juice.
3. Set the crock-pot on low and cook for about 8 hours.
4. Dish out and serve hot.

Nutritional Value:

- *Calories 309*
- *Total Fat 12.1 g*
- *Saturated Fat 3.6 g*
- *Cholesterol 137 mg*
- *Total Carbs 1.6 g*
- *Sugar 0.7 g*
- *Fiber 0.8 g*
- *Sodium 201 mg*
- *Potassium 390 mg*
- *Protein 45.8 g*

Creamy Turkey Breast

Preparation Time: 10 minutes
Cooking Time: 15 minutes
Servings: 6
Ingredients:

- 2 tablespoons butter
- 1½ cups Italian dressing
- 1 (2-pound) bone-in turkey breast
- 2 garlic cloves, minced
- Salt and freshly ground black pepper, to taste

Method:

1. Preheat the oven to 350 degrees F and grease a baking dish with butter.
2. Mix together minced garlic cloves, salt and black pepper and rub the turkey breast with this mixture.
3. Arrange turkey breast in the baking dish and top evenly with Italian dressing.
4. Bake for about 2 hours, coating with pan juices occasionally.
5. Dish out and serve immediately.

Nutritional Value:

- *Calories 369*
- *Total Fat 23.2 g*
- *Saturated Fat 5.1 g*
- *Cholesterol 104 mg*
- *Total Carbs 6.5 g*
- *Sugar 4.9 g*
- *Fiber 0 g*
- *Sodium 990 mg*
- *Potassium 33 mg*
- *Protein 35.4 g*

Caprese Hassel back Chicken

Preparation Time: 10 minutes
Cooking Time: 15 minutes
Servings: 4
Ingredients:

- 4 large chicken breasts
- 2 tablespoons butter
- 1 cup fresh mozzarella cheese, thinly sliced
- 2 large roma tomatoes, thinly sliced
- Salt and freshly ground black pepper, to taste

Method:

1. Make some deep slits in the chicken breasts and season with salt and black pepper.
2. Stuff the tomatoes and mozzarella cheese slices in the chicken slits.
3. Preheat the oven to 360 degrees F and grease the baking dish with butter.
4. Put the stuffed chicken breasts in the baking tray and transfer into the oven.
5. Bake for about 1 hour and dish out.

Nutritional Value:

- *Calories 287*
- *Total Fat 15 g*
- *Saturated Fat 6.6 g*
- *Cholesterol 112 mg*
- *Total Carbs 3.8 g*
- *Sugar 2.4 g*
- *Fiber 1.1 g*
- *Sodium 178 mg*
- *Potassium 473 mg*
- *Protein 33.2 g*

Mediterranean Turkey Cutlets

Preparation Time: 10 minutes
Cooking Time: 15 minutes
Servings: 4
Ingredients:

- 1-pound turkey cutlets
- 1 teaspoon Greek seasoning
- 2 tablespoons olive oil
- ½ cup almond flour
- 1 teaspoon turmeric powder

Method:

1. Mix together almond flour, Greek seasoning and turmeric powder in a bowl and dredge turkey cutlets in it.
2. Keep aside for about 15 minutes.
3. Heat oil in a skillet and transfer half of the turkey cutlets.
4. Cover the lid and cook for about 20 minutes on medium-low heat.
5. Dish out in a serving platter.

Nutritional Value:

- *Calories 340*
- *Total Fat 19.4 g*
- *Saturated Fat 3.4 g*
- *Cholesterol 86 mg*
- *Total Carbs 3.7 g*
- *Sugar 0 g*
- *Fiber 1.6 g*
- *Sodium 124 mg*
- *Potassium 356 mg*
- *Protein 36.3 g*

Keto Garlic Turkey Breasts

Preparation Time: 10 minutes
Cooking Time: 15 minutes
Servings: 4
Ingredients:

- 4 tablespoons butter
- ½ teaspoon garlic powder
- ¼ teaspoon dried oregano
- ½ teaspoon salt
- 1-pound turkey breasts, boneless
- ¼ teaspoon dried basil
- 1 teaspoon black pepper

Method:

1. Sprinkle seasonings on both sides of the turkey.
2. Put butter in a skillet and add seasoned turkey.
3. Cook for about 4 minutes on each side and dish out.
4. Preheat the oven to 450 degrees F and transfer the turkey in it.
5. Bake for about 15 minutes and dish out in a platter.

Nutritional Value:

- *Calories 223*
- *Total Fat 13.4 g*
- *Saturated Fat 7.7 g*
- *Cholesterol 79 mg*
- *Total Carbs 5.4 g*
- *Sugar 4.1 g*
- *Fiber 0.8 g*
- *Sodium 1524 mg*
- *Potassium 358 mg*
- *Protein 19.6 g*

Chili Lime Turkey

Preparation Time: 10 minutes
Cooking Time: 10 minutes
Servings: 6
Ingredients:

- 1 onion, diced
- ¼ cup cooking wine
- 1 teaspoon sea salt
- ½ cup organic chicken broth
- ½ teaspoon paprika
- 2 pounds turkey thighs
- 5 garlic cloves, minced
- 1 teaspoon dried parsley
- 1 tablespoon lime juice
- 3 green chilies, chopped
- ¼ cup butter

Directions:

1. Heat butter in a large skillet and add onions and garlic.
2. Sauté for about 3 minutes and add rest of the ingredients.
3. Cook for about 20 minutes and transfer to a platter.

Nutritional Value:

- *Calories 282*
- *Total Fat 15.2 g*
- *Saturated Fat 7.2 g*
- *Cholesterol 129 mg*
- *Total Carbs 6.3 g*
- *Sugar 3.3 g*
- *Fiber 0.9 g*
- *Sodium 2117 mg*
- *Potassium 511 mg*
- *Protein 27.4 g*

CHAPTER12: SEAFOOD RECIPES

Salmon Stew

Preparation Time: 5 minutes
Cooking Time: 12 minutes
Servings: 3
Ingredients:

- 1 medium onion, chopped
- 1 cup homemade fish broth
- 1-pound salmon fillet, cubed
- 1 tablespoon butter
- Salt and freshly ground black pepper, to taste

Method:

1. Season the salmon fillets with salt and black pepper.
2. Heat butter in a skillet and add onions.
3. Sauté for about 3 minutes and add salmon.
4. Cook for about 2 minutes on each side and stir in fish broth.
5. Cover the lid and cook for about 7 minutes.
6. Dish out and serve hot.

Nutritional Value:

- *Calories 272*
- *Total Fat 14.2 g*
- *Saturated Fat 4.1 g*
- *Cholesterol 82 mg*
- *Total Carbs 4.4 g*
- *Sugar 1.9 g*
- *Fiber 1.1 g*
- *Sodium 275 mg*
- *Potassium 635 mg*
- *Protein 32.1 g*

Paprika Shrimp

Preparation Time: 5 minutes
Cooking Time: 20 minutes
Servings: 6
Ingredients:

- 6 tablespoons butter
- 1 teaspoon smoked paprika
- 2 pounds tiger shrimps
- Salt, to taste

Method:

1. Preheat the oven to 400 degrees F and grease a baking dish with butter.
2. Mix together all the ingredients in a large bowl and marinate the shrimp in it.
3. Place the seasoned shrimp in the baking dish and transfer the baking dish in oven.
4. Bake for about 15 minutes and dish out.

Nutritional Value:

- *Calories 173*
- *Total Fat 8.3 g*
- *Saturated Fat 1.3 g*
- *Cholesterol 221 mg*
- *Total Carbs 0.1 g*
- *Sugar 0 g*
- *Fiber 0.1 g*
- *Sodium 332 mg*
- *Potassium 212 mg*
- *Protein 23.8 g*

Ketogenic Butter Fish

Preparation Time: 10 minutes
Cooking Time: 30 minutes
Servings: 3
Ingredients:

- 3 green chilies, chopped
- 2 tablespoons ginger-garlic paste
- 1-pound salmon fillets
- ¾ cup butter
- Salt and freshly ground black pepper, to taste

Method:

1. Season the salmon fillets with ginger-garlic paste, salt and black pepper.
2. Place the salmon fillets in the pot and top with green chilies and butter.
3. Cook on low heat for about 30 minutes and dish out.

Nutritional Value:

- *Calories 507*
- *Total Fat 45.9 g*
- *Saturated Fat 22.9 g*
- *Cholesterol 142 mg*
- *Total Carbs 2.4 g*
- *Sugar 0.2 g*
- *Fiber 0.1 g*
- *Sodium 296 mg*
- *Potassium 453 mg*
- *Protein 22.8 g*

Shrimp Magic

Preparation Time: 10 minutes
Cooking Time: 15 minutes
Servings: 3
Ingredients:

- ½ teaspoon smoked paprika
- 2 tablespoons butter
- 1-pound shrimps, peeled and deveined
- 1 red chili pepper, seeded and chopped
- Lemongrass stalks

Method:

1. Mix together all the ingredients in a bowl except lemongrass and marinate for about 2 hours.
2. Preheat the oven to 390 degrees F and thread the shrimps onto lemongrass stalks.
3. Bake for about 15 minutes and serve immediately.

Nutritional Value:

- *Calories 251*
- *Total Fat 10.3 g*
- *Saturated Fat 5.7 g*
- *Cholesterol 339 mg*
- *Total Carbs 3 g*
- *Sugar 0.1 g*
- *Fiber 0.2 g*
- *Sodium 424 mg*
- *Potassium 281 mg*
- *Protein 34.6 g*

Sweet and Sour Fish

Preparation Time: 10 minutes
Cooking Time: 15 minutes
Servings: 3
Ingredients:

- 2 drops liquid stevia
- ¼ cup butter
- 1-pound fish chunks
- 1 tablespoon vinegar
- Salt and freshly ground black pepper, to taste

Method:

1. Melt the butter in a large skillet and add fish chunks.
2. Cook for about 3 minutes and add stevia.
3. Cook for about 1 minute and add salt and black pepper.
4. Stir continuously for about 10 minutes at medium-low heat.
5. Dish out in a serving bowl and serve immediately.

Nutritional Value:

- *Calories 274*
- *Total Fat 15.4 g*
- *Saturated Fat 9.7 g*
- *Cholesterol 54 mg*
- *Total Carbs 2.8 g*
- *Sugar 0 g*
- *Fiber 0 g*
- *Sodium 604 mg*
- *Potassium 8 mg*
- *Protein 33.2 g*

Buttered Scallops

Preparation Time: 10 minutes
Cooking Time: 15 minutes
Servings: 6
Ingredients:

- 4 garlic cloves, minced
- 4 tablespoons fresh rosemary, chopped
- 2 pounds sea scallops
- ½ cup butter
- Salt and freshly ground black pepper, to taste

Method:

1. Heat butter on medium-high heat in a medium skillet and add rosemary and garlic.
2. Sauté for about 1 minute and stir in the sea scallops, salt and black pepper.
3. Cook for about 2 minutes on each side and dish out.
4. Add garlic and rosemary and sauté for about 1 minute.
5. Stir in the sea scallops, salt and black pepper and cook for about 2 minutes on each side.
6. Dish out and serve hot.

Nutritional Value:

- *Calories 279*
- *Total Fat 16.8 g*
- *Saturated Fat 10 g*
- *Cholesterol 91 mg*
- *Total Carbs 5.7 g*
- *Sugar 0 g*
- *Fiber 1 g*
- *Sodium 354 mg*
- *Potassium 520 mg*
- *Protein 25.8 g*

Buffalo Fish

Preparation Time: 10 minutes
Cooking Time: 9 minutes
Servings: 3
Ingredients:

- 1/3 cup Franks red hot sauce
- 3 tablespoons butter
- 3 fish fillets
- 1 teaspoon garlic powder
- Salt and freshly ground black pepper, to taste

Method:

1. Heat butter in a large skillet and add fish fillets.
2. Cook for about 2 minutes on each side and add salt, black pepper and garlic powder.
3. Cook for about 1 minute and add Franks red hot sauce.
4. Cover the lid and cook for about 6 minutes on low heat.
5. Dish out in a serving platter and serve hot.

Nutritional Value:

- Calories 317
- Total Fat 22.7 g
- Saturated Fat 9.9 g
- Cholesterol 61 mg
- Total Carbs 16.4 g
- Sugar 0.2 g
- Fiber 0.6 g
- Sodium 659 mg
- Potassium 307 mg
- Protein 13.6 g

Cod: Battle of Herbs

Preparation Time: 5 minutes
Cooking Time: 8 minutes
Servings: 3
Ingredients:

- 6 eggs
- 4 garlic cloves, minced
- 2 small onions, chopped finely
- 2 teaspoons soy sauce
- 3 (4-ounce) skinless cod fish fillets, cut into rectangular pieces
- ¼ cup butter
- 2 green chilies, chopped finely
- Salt and freshly ground black pepper, to taste

Method:

1. Put all the ingredients except cod in a shallow dish and beat well.
2. Dip each fillet in this mixture and keep aside.
3. Preheat the Air fryer to 375 degrees F and place the fish in an Air fryer basket.
4. Cook for about 8 minutes and dish out.

Nutritional Value:

- *Calories 409*
- *Total Fat 25.2 g*
- *Saturated Fat 12.6 g*
- *Cholesterol 430 mg*
- *Total Carbs 7 g*
- *Sugar 3 g*
- *Fiber 1.1 g*
- *Sodium 363 mg*
- *Potassium 483 mg*
- *Protein 37.9 g*

CHAPTER13: SOUPS RECIPES

Cheesy Broccoli Soup

Preparation Time: 10 minutes
Cooking Time: 4 hours
Servings: 6
Ingredients:

- 2 cups chicken broth
- 1 cup heavy whipping cream
- 2 cups broccoli
- 2 cups cheddar cheese
- Salt, to taste

Method:

1. Stir in the broccoli, cheddar cheese, chicken broth, salt and heavy whipping cream in a slow cooker.
2. Set the slow cooker on low and cook for about 4 hours.
3. Dish out and serve hot.

Nutritional Value:

- Calories 244
- Total Fat 20.4 g
- Saturated Fat 67 g
- Cholesterol 130 mg
- Total Carbs 3.4 g
- Sugar 1 g
- Fiber 0.8 g
- Sodium 506 mg
- Potassium 217 mg
- Protein 12.3 g

Healthy Chicken Soup

Preparation Time: 10 minutes
Cooking Time: 10 minutes
Servings: 4
Ingredients:

- 3 celery stalks, chopped
- 4 cups homemade chicken broth
- 1 small yellow onion, chopped
- 1 cup water
- 1-pound grass-fed cooked chicken, shredded
- 2 tablespoons olive oil
- ¼ teaspoon dried oregano, crushed
- 2 cups fresh spinach, trimmed and chopped
- ¼ teaspoon dried thyme, crushed
- Salt and freshly ground black pepper, to taste

Method:

1. Put the olive oil in a pressure cooker and add celery and onions.
2. Cook for about 5 minutes and add herbs and black pepper.
3. Cook for about 1 minute and add broth and water.
4. Close the lid and cook for about 5 minutes at high pressure.
5. Quickly release the pressure and stir in the spinach and chicken.
6. Cook for about 2 more minutes and dish out.

Nutritional Value:

- *Calories 296*
- *Total Fat 11.9 g*
- *Saturated Fat 2.4 g*
- *Cholesterol 87 mg*
- *Total Carbs 6.5 g*
- *Sugar 1.6 g*
- *Fiber 1.1 g*
- *Sodium 862 mg*
- *Potassium 644 mg*

- Protein 39 g

Bacon and Veggie Soup

Preparation Time: 10 minutes
Cooking Time: 10 minutes
Servings: 4

Ingredients:

- 1 small yellow onion, chopped
- 2 garlic cloves, minced
- 1 cup half-and-half
- 4 dashes hot pepper sauce
- 6 cooked turkey bacon slices, chopped
- 1 head cauliflower, chopped roughly
- 2 cups Cheddar cheese, shredded
- 1 tablespoon olive oil
- 4 cups homemade chicken broth
- Freshly ground black pepper, to taste

Method:

1. Put the olive oil in the pot and add garlic and onions.
2. Cook for about 3 minutes and add cauliflower, broth, salt and black pepper.
3. Cover the lid and cook for about 20 minutes on medium-low heat.
4. Open the lid and add remaining ingredients.
5. Cook for about 5 minutes and dish out.

Nutritional Value:

- *Calories 424*
- *Total Fat 31.4 g*
- *Saturated Fat 17.1 g*
- *Cholesterol 97 mg*
- *Total Carbs 8.2 g*
- *Sugar 2.7 g*
- *Fiber 1.7 g*
- *Sodium 1339 mg*
- *Potassium 547 mg*
- *Protein 26.6 g*

Omega-3 Rich Salmon Soup

Preparation Time: 15 minutes
Cooking Time: 13 minutes
Servings: 4
Ingredients:

- 1-pound salmon fillets
- 1 tablespoon olive oil
- ½ cup celery stalk, chopped
- ½ cup yellow onion, chopped
- 1 cup cauliflower, chopped
- 2 cups homemade chicken broth
- Salt and freshly ground black pepper, to taste
- ¼ cup fresh parsley, chopped

Method:

1. Arrange the steamer basket in the bottom of the pressure cooker and add 1 cup of water.
2. Place the salmon fillets on steamer basket in a single layer.
3. Lock the lid and cook for about 8-9 minutes at high pressure.
4. Quickly release the pressure and transfer the salmon onto a plate, cutting it into bite sized pieces.
5. Put the oil in the pressure cooker and add celery and onions.
6. Cook for about 3 minutes and add salmon pieces.
7. Dish out and serve hot.

Nutritional Value:

- *Calories 215*
- *Total Fat 11.3 g*
- *Saturated Fat 1.7 g*
- *Cholesterol 50 mg*
- *Total Carbs 3.8 g*
- *Sugar 1.8 g*
- *Fiber 1.3 g*
- *Sodium 452 mg*
- *Potassium 689 mg*

- *Protein 25.3 g*

Cheesy Vegetable Soup

Preparation Time: 10 minutes
Cooking Time: 20 minutes
Servings: 5
Ingredients:

- ½ small yellow onion, chopped
- 1 cup Parmesan cheese, grated
- 1 cup Muenster cheese, grated
- 1 cup Swiss cheese, grated
- ½ tablespoon garlic, minced
- 3 cups homemade vegetable broth
- ½ teaspoon dried thyme, crushed
- 2 cups cauliflower, chopped
- 1 teaspoon olive oil
- ½ pound fresh Baby Bella mushrooms, chopped

Method:

1. Put the olive oil in the pressure cooker and add garlic and onions.
2. Cook for about 3 minutes and stir in the mushrooms.
3. Cook for about 5 minutes and add cauliflower and broth.
4. Lock the lid and cook for about 5 minutes at high pressure.
5. Naturally release the pressure and puree the soup with an immersion blender.
6. Return the soup in the cooker and add Parmesan cheese.
7. Cook for about 5 minutes and serve simmering hot.

Nutritional Value:

- *Calories 226*
- *Total Fat 15.1 g*
- *Saturated Fat 9.1 g*
- *Cholesterol 46 mg*
- *Total Carbs 6.8 g*
- *Sugar 3.8 g*
- *Fiber 2.5 g*
- *Sodium 569 mg*

- Potassium 402 mg
- Protein 15 g

Mexican Inspired Beef Soup

Preparation Time: 15 minutes
Cooking Time: 15 minutes
Servings: 4

Ingredients:

- 1-pound grass-fed lean ground beef
- 4-ounce cream cheese
- 2 cups homemade beef broth
- 1 tablespoon chili powder
- Salt and freshly ground black pepper, to taste
- ¼ cup cheddar cheese, shredded
- ½ teaspoon olive oil
- 10-ounce canned sugar-free diced tomatoes with green chilies
- ¼ cup heavy cream
- 2 garlic cloves, minced
- 1 teaspoon ground cumin

Method:

1. Place the oil in the Instant Pot and select "Sauté". Then add the beef and cook for about 8-10 minutes. Drain excess grease from pot.
2. Select "Cancel" and stir in the remaining ingredients except cheddar cheese.
3. Secure the lid and select "Soup" and just use the default time of 5 minutes.
4. Select the "Cancel" and carefully do a Natural release.
5. Serve hot with the topping of cheddar cheese.

Nutritional Value:

- *Calories 405*
- *Total Fat 26.7 g*
- *Saturated Fat 14.3 g*
- *Cholesterol 124 mg*
- *Total Carbs 6.7 g*
- *Sugar 3.5 g*
- *Fiber 1.9 g*
- *Sodium 815 mg*

- *Potassium 385 mg*
- *Protein 31.1 g*

Tomato Soup

Preparation Time: 15 minutes
Cooking Time: 15 minutes
Servings: 4
Ingredients:

- 1 teaspoon dried basil, crushed
- 2 cups low-sodium vegetable broth
- 2 tablespoons Erythritol
- ½ tablespoon balsamic vinegar
- ¼ cup fresh basil, chopped
- ½ tablespoon olive oil
- 1 garlic clove, minced
- 1-pound fresh tomatoes, chopped
- 1 teaspoon dried parsley, crushed
- 1 cup cheddar cheese
- Freshly ground black pepper, to taste

Method:

1. Put the oil in a pot and add garlic, tomatoes, herbs, black pepper and broth.
2. Cover the lid and cook for about 20 minutes on medium-low heat.
3. Stir in sugar and vinegar and puree the soup with an immersion blender.
4. Garnish with basil and serve immediately.

Nutritional Value:

- *Calories 194*
- *Total Fat 15.4 g*
- *Saturated Fat 9.6 g*
- *Cholesterol 45 mg*
- *Total Carbs 5.6 g*
- *Sugar 3.2 g*
- *Fiber 1.4 g*
- *Sodium 257 mg*
- *Potassium 305 mg*
- *Protein 9.2 g*

Kale and Chicken Soup

Preparation Time: 10 minutes
Cooking Time: 12 minutes
Servings: 5
Ingredients:

- 1 medium onion, chopped
- ¼ teaspoon dried oregano, crushed
- Freshly ground black pepper, to taste
- 1-pound cooked chicken, shredded
- 2 cups fresh kale, trimmed and chopped
- ½ teaspoon Worcestershire sauce
- 4 tablespoons butter
- 1 cup Parmesan cheese
- ½ cup heavy whipping cream
- 2 bay leaves
- ¼ teaspoon dried thyme, crushed
- 4 cups low-sodium chicken broth
- 1 cup water

Method:

1. Put the butter in the pressure cooker and add celery and onions.
2. Cook for about 5 minutes and add herbs, bay leaves and black pepper.
3. Cook for about 1 minute and add broth and water.
4. Lock the lid and cook for about 5 minutes at high pressure.
5. Quickly release the pressure and stir in the kale, chicken and cheese.
6. Cook for about 2 more minutes and pour in Worcestershire sauce.

Nutritional Value:

- *Calories 314*
- *Total Fat 17.7 g*
- *Saturated Fat 10.2 g*
- *Cholesterol 115 mg*
- *Total Carbs 6.6 g*
- *Sugar 1.1 g*

- Fiber 1 g
- Sodium 255 mg
- Potassium 359 mg
- Protein 31.1 g

CHAPTER14: DESSERTS RECIPES

Chocolate Peanut Butter Cups

Preparation Time: 10 minutes
Cooking Time: 4 hours
Servings: 3
Ingredients:

- ¼ cup heavy cream
- 1 cup butter
- 2 ounces unsweetened chocolate
- 4 packets stevia
- ¼ cup peanut butter, separated

Method:

1. Preheat the oven to 360 degrees F and melt the butter and peanut butter in a bowl.
2. Stir in unsweetened chocolate, stevia and heavy cream.
3. Mix thoroughly and pour the mixture in a baking mold.
4. Put the baking mold in the oven and bake for about 30 minutes.

Nutritional Value:

- *Calories 479*
- *Total Fat 51.5 g*
- *Saturated Fat 29.7 g*
- *Cholesterol 106 mg*
- *Total Carbs 7.7 g*
- *Sugar 1.4 g*
- *Fiber 2.7 g*
- *Sodium 69 mg*
- *Potassium 193 mg*
- *Protein 5.2 g*

Crème Brûlée

Preparation Time: 10 minutes
Cooking Time: 15 minutes
Servings: 4
Ingredients:

- ½ tablespoon vanilla extract
- 1 cup heavy cream
- 3 egg yolks
- ¼ cup stevia
- 1 pinch salt

Method:

1. Preheat the oven to 395 degrees F.
2. Combine together vanilla extract, egg yolks, salt and heavy cream in a bowl and beat until well mixed.
3. Divide the mixture evenly into 4 greased ramekins.
4. Transfer the ramekins in the oven and bake for about 15 minutes.
5. Cover the ramekins with a plastic wrap and refrigerate to chill for about 2 hours.

Nutritional Value:

- *Calories 149*
- *Total Fat 14.5 g*
- *Saturated Fat 8.1 g*
- *Cholesterol 56 mg*
- *Total Carbs 1.6 g*
- *Sugar 0.3 g*
- *Fiber 0 g*
- *Sodium 56 mg*
- *Potassium 39 mg*
- *Protein 2.6 g*

Flourless Chocolate Brownies

Preparation Time: 10 minutes
Cooking Time: 30 minutes
Servings: 4
Ingredients:

- ½ cup butter
- 3 eggs
- ½ cup sugar-free chocolate chips
- 1 teaspoon vanilla extract
- 2 scoops stevia

Directions:

1. Preheat the oven to 390 degrees F and grease a baking mold.
2. Whisk together eggs and add stevia and vanilla extract.
3. Put the eggs mixture in the blender and blend until frothy.
4. Put the butter and chocolate in a pan and melt on low heat.
5. Add the melted chocolate mixture to the egg mixture.
6. Pour it in the baking mold and transfer the baking mold in the oven.
7. Bake for about 30 minutes and dish out.
8. Cut into square pieces and serve with whipped cream.

Nutritional Information per Serving:

- *Calories 266*
- *Total Fat 26.9 g*
- *Saturated Fat 15.8 g*
- *Cholesterol 184 mg*
- *Total Carbs 2.5 g*
- *Sugar 0.4 g*
- *Fiber 0 g*
- *Sodium 218 mg*
- *Potassium 53 mg*
- *Protein 4.5 g*

Cream Crepes

Preparation Time: 10 minutes
Cooking Time: 16 minutes
Servings: 4

Ingredients:

- 2 organic eggs
- 1 teaspoon Splenda
- 2 tablespoons coconut flour
- 2 tablespoons coconut oil, melted and divided
- 1/3 cup heavy cream

Method:

1. Mix together 1 tablespoon of coconut oil, eggs, Splenda and salt in a bowl and beat until well combined.
2. Add the coconut flour slowly and beat continuously.
3. Stir in the heavy cream and continuously beat until well mixed.
4. Heat a non-stick pan and pour about ¼ of the mixture in it.
5. Cook for about 2 minutes on each side.
6. Repeat with the remaining mixture in three batches and serve with additional whipped cream.

Nutritional Value:

- *Calories 145*
- *Total Fat 13.1 g*
- *Saturated Fat 9.1 g*
- *Cholesterol 96 mg*
- *Total Carbs 4 g*
- *Sugar 1.2 g*
- *Fiber 1.5 g*
- *Sodium 35 mg*
- *Potassium 37 mg*
- *Protein 3.5 g*

Nut Porridge

Preparation Time: 10 minutes
Cooking Time: 10 minutes
Servings: 4
Ingredients:

- 1 cup pecan, halved
- 4 teaspoons coconut oil, melted
- 2 cups water
- 1 cup cashew nuts, raw and unsalted
- 2 tablespoons stevia

Method:

1. Put the pecans and cashew nuts in the food processor and pulse until chunked.
2. Put the nuts mixture into the pot and stir in water, coconut oil and stevia.
3. Cook for about 5 minutes on high heat and then lower the flame.
4. Simmer for about 10 minutes on low heat and serve.

Nutritional Value:

- *Calories 260*
- *Total Fat 22.9 g*
- *Saturated Fat 7.3 g*
- *Cholesterol 0 mg*
- *Total Carbs 12.7 g*
- *Sugar 1.8 g*
- *Fiber 1.4 g*
- *Sodium 9 mg*
- *Potassium 209 mg*
- *Protein 5.6 g*

Lemon Mousse

Preparation Time: 10 minutes
Cooking Time: 12 minutes
Servings: 2
Ingredients:

- ½ cup heavy cream
- 4-ounce cream cheese, softened
- 1/8 cup fresh lemon juice
- 2 pinches salt
- ½ teaspoon lemon liquid stevia

Method:

1. Preheat the oven to 350 degrees F and grease 2 ramekins.
2. Mix together heavy cream, cream cheese, fresh lemon juice, salt and lemon liquid stevia in a bowl.
3. Pour into the ramekins and transfer the ramekins into the oven.
4. Bake for about 12 minutes and pour into the serving glasses.
5. Refrigerate for at least 3 hours and chill before serving.

Nutritional Value:

- *Calories 305*
- *Total Fat 31 g*
- *Saturated Fat 19.5 g*
- *Cholesterol 103 mg*
- *Total Carbs 2.7 g*
- *Sugar 0.5 g*
- *Fiber 0.1 g*
- *Sodium 299 mg*
- *Potassium 109 mg*
- *Protein 5 g*

Chocolate Cheese Cake

Preparation Time: 10 minutes
Cooking Time: 12 minutes
Servings: 6
Ingredients:

- 2 cups cream cheese, softened
- 2 eggs
- 2 tablespoons cocoa powder
- 1 teaspoon pure vanilla extract
- ½ cup swerve

Method:

1. Preheat the oven to 350 degrees F.
2. Put eggs and cream cheese in an immersion blender and blend until smooth.
3. Pour in the vanilla extract, cocoa powder and swerve.
4. Pulse until well mixed and transfer the mixture evenly into 2 (8-ounce) mason jars.
5. Put the mason jars in the oven and bake for about 12 minutes.
6. Refrigerate for at least 3 hours before serving and serve chilled.

Nutritional Value:

- *Calories 244*
- *Total Fat 24.8 g*
- *Saturated Fat 15.6 g*
- *Cholesterol 32 mg*
- *Total Carbs 2.1 g*
- *Sugar 0.4 g*
- *Fiber 0.1 g*
- *Sodium 204 mg*
- *Potassium 81 mg*
- *Protein 4 g*

Vanilla Yogurt

Preparation Time: 20 minutes
Cooking Time: 6 hours
Servings: 2
Ingredients:

- ¼ cup yogurt starter
- ½ cup full-fat milk
- 1 cup heavy cream
- 2 scoops stevia
- ½ tablespoon pure vanilla extract

Directions:

1. Pour milk into the slow cooker and put it on low for about 3 hours.
2. Whisk in heavy cream, vanilla extract and stevia and allow the yogurt to sit.
3. Set the slow cooker on low and cook for about 3 hours.
4. Stir in the yogurt starter in 1 cup of milk.
5. Return this mixture to the slow cooker and mix well.
6. Put the lid back on the slow cooker and wrap the slow cooker in two small towels.
7. Let the wrapped slow cooker sit for about 9 hours and allow the yogurt to culture.
8. Dish out in a serving bowl or store it by refrigerating.

Nutritional Value:

- *Calories 292*
- *Total Fat 26.2 g*
- *Saturated Fat 16.3 g*
- *Cholesterol 100 mg*
- *Total Carbs 8.2 g*
- *Sugar 6.6 g*
- *Fiber 0 g*
- *Sodium 86 mg*
- *Potassium 250 mg*
- *Protein 5.2 g*

Conclusion:

The keto plan is basically based on ketosis. Ketosis basically changes the body metabolism from using glucose as an energy source to ketones or fat burning. Ketosis can be achieved with a steady pace and has different stages which are defined by the ketone levels present in the body. This diet plan has been credited with a lot of advantages like weight loss, enhanced mental and physical capabilities, reversal and treatment of type 2 diabetes, treating Alzheimer's disease, epilepsy and caner. It has also been experimented for treatment of Parkinson's disease. It does come with a few side effects in the beginning but they are temporary and fade away as soon as your body gets adjusted to the ketogenic diet plan.

For having a successful ketogenic life style one should reduce the intake of carbohydrates. Improve fat consumption, reduce proteins and remain hydrated. The diet plan should be calculated prior to converting on the ketogenic to avoid any hardships. The ketogenic diet plan is easy to follow and have meals from almost every food category and for every occasion. A wide range of healthy and delicious breakfasts, lunches, dinners, snacks and desserts can be prepared using ketogenic recipes. In case of medical complication like cramps or constipation etc., one should immediately consult a physician for expert opinion for any alterations to the diet plan.

The keto plan is very efficient and its effectiveness varies from person to person. The keto plan has to be followed on a regular basis to maintain your health and physical attire, the moment you stop following it will be the moment you will start your journey back from you started in the first place. The keto plan is not that much costly and wit a few methods you can prevent it becoming a burden on your budget.

Lightning Source UK Ltd.
Milton Keynes UK
UKHW05f0222250718
326224UK00003B/210/P

9 781720 668824